Table of Contents

Introduction 1

Historical Recipes 2

Posters 41

Cocktails 51

Disclaimer 59

Author's Note 60

Если вы не пьете, вы умрете здоровым

‘If you don’t drink, you’ll die healthy’

Between 1979 and 1989 over 620,000 Soviet soldiers passed through Afghanistan. Likened to a Soviet Vietnam, the war in Afghanistan would shake Soviet society to its core and destroy countless lives. Life for those selected for internationalist service was often austere.

Many needed a drink.

Using historical data, interviews and other primary sources, this cocktail book illustrates the cunning creativity of the Russian conscripts who ingeniously—and often fatally—discovered new ways to get trashed.

The following case studies explore how these ‘battlefield chemists’ and traumatized alcoholics got their fix.

Mixed drinks inspired by these accounts and those rooted within wider Soviet alcoholic innovation are works of historical fiction.

Голь на вы́думку хитра́
‘Poverty inspires invention’

HISTORICAL RECIPES

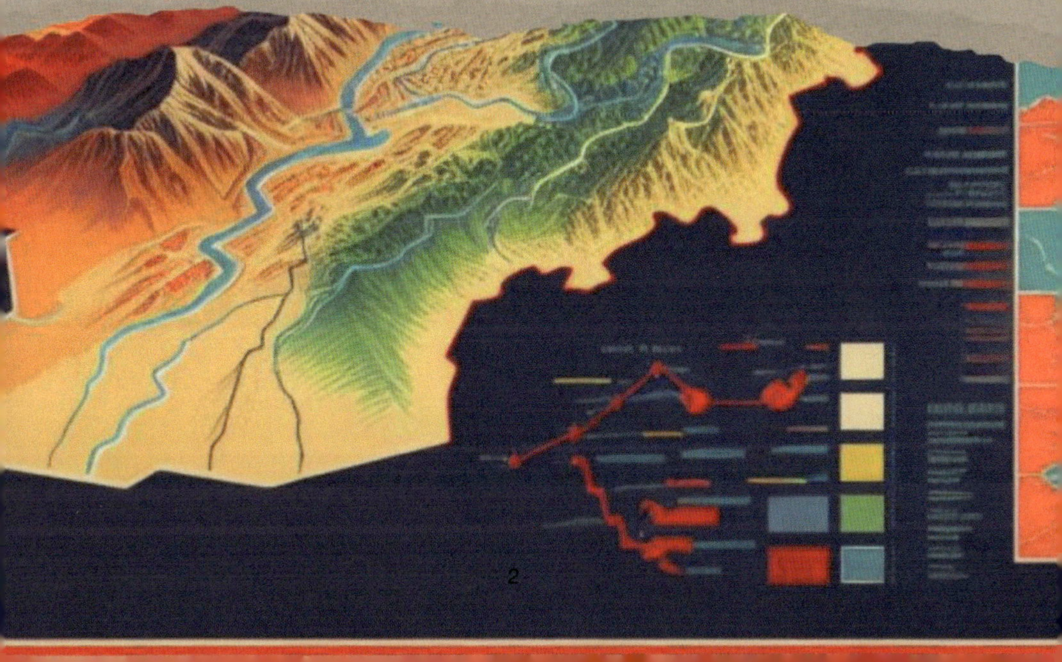

Eau de Cologne

Alcohol Content: 70-90% ethanol

A scented refreshment with a high alcohol content enjoyed by conscripts and officers alike. It was common for some to drink a bottle or two per day.

Cologne

Cost: 98 Kopeks

Vodka

Cost: 10+ Rubles

Method

Stronger smelling cologne and perfumes were often drank straight (in shot form) while more palatable scents like 'Lily of the Valley' (considered neutral, sweet, and reliable) were used in cocktails. Sugar and sweets were used as chasers.

> 'One army doctor recounted to me a tale of having to operate on a soldier hit by shrapnel from a rebel mortar, whose innards still smelled of cheap cologne.' - Prof Mark Galeotti

Chifir

Alcohol Content: **0%**

An extremely strong tea, widely used by GULAG prisoners and those wishing to offset the effects of hunger and exhaustion.

Fact: During the brewing process, the leaves start to release adenine and guanine into the water, which does not happen during traditional tea-making.

Method

Typically prepared with 5–8 tablespoons (50–100 ml) of loose tea (or tea bags) per person poured on top of the boiled water. Brew for a long time, and sip slowly to avoid vomiting. It's very bitter.

> ‘Strong excitement is felt, the illusion of a surge of strength, expansion of consciousness is created, a person begins to ’see more.’ - Anonymous

Samagon

Alcohol Content: **40%+**

Translating to 'self made' Samagon is a Moonshine, made widely in rural areas but consumed by all.

Fact: The Soviet Union's purchase of beet sugar from Cuba accelerated the growth of Samagon production -undermining prohibition efforts in the 1980s.

Method

'Take a big pot with bread, water, a lot of sugar, and a bit of yeast. Heat the mix. The vapor first rises and then condenses because it's sent through a pipe that's cooled down by water or ice. The vapor comes out as little drops on the other end. The traditional method is to collect the drops in a jar. It's a small jar to begin with because the spirit is not any good at that stage. Every half hour or so you push a piece of paper or cloth into the liquid and light it on fire. If the flame's still red, your eyes will be dead. Once the flame reaches a solid blue, it's drinkable.' - Andre Simonov

> "'It is thicker than water and a bit like clouded jelly. It tastes like shit and can make you blind.'
> - Andre Simonov, *Vice*"

"A shameful union — a slacker and vodka!"

Brake Fluid

Alcohol Content: 49%+

A beverage to lubricate your car and your body. Contains 'technical alcohol' - not to be consumed.

(49% alcohol) (49% distilled water) (1% triethanolamine phosphate) (1% sodium mercaptobenzothiazole)

Fact: Consumption makes it harder to break. In 1982, a Soviet truck collided with a fuel tanker in the Salang Tunnel - killing hundreds.

*Afghan insurgents denied any role in the tunnel explosion

Method

- In cold weather, put the fluid in a pan or pipe out in the cold. Let it freeze over. It was believed that the additives would freeze to the metal while the alcohol could be poured out.

- Filter through bread. Add raisins and sugar to the separated alcohol. Put out to ferment for a few days and enjoy.

> 'The reality was being stuck in a tank with our machine guns poking out left and right. We were like a great iron hedgehog'
> - Private (Signals Corps), *Zinky Boys*

Antifreeze

Alcohol Content: **47-50%**

Antifreeze is typically ethylene glycol, plus a little water. Or, in some cases, a lot of water.

Fact: Ethylene glycol is an odorless, colorless, flammable, viscous liquid. It has a sweet taste but is toxic in high concentrations.

Early symptoms of poisoning mimic those of alcohol.

Method

Boil the antifreeze. At 100°C water boils off and you're left with ethylene glycol, which boils at 200°C.

Nearly impossible to distill in field conditions.
Normally drank straight.
The consequences were severe and often fatal.

> 'We'd warn new recruits not to touch antifreeze, whatever else they drank, but within a few days they'd be in hospital with their insides corroded.'
> - Anonymous (RAND Interview)

антифриз

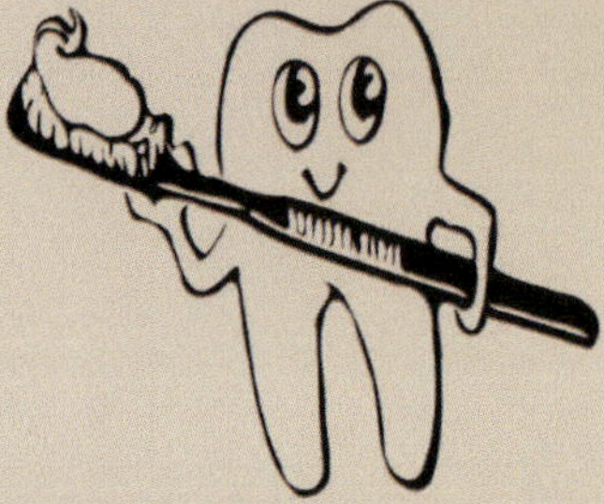

Toothpaste

Alcohol Content: 2-5%

A widely available but less effective source of technical alcohol.

Fact: The Bulgarian Pomorin Brand was popular- having both a higher alcohol content than other pastes and being widely available. The paste tasted 'salty' and contained Pomorie liquor.

Method

- Squeeze four or five tubes into a jar, dilute it with water, and drink.
- Spread on bread and wait. Eventually, a gunk will form. Scrape it off and eat the bread.

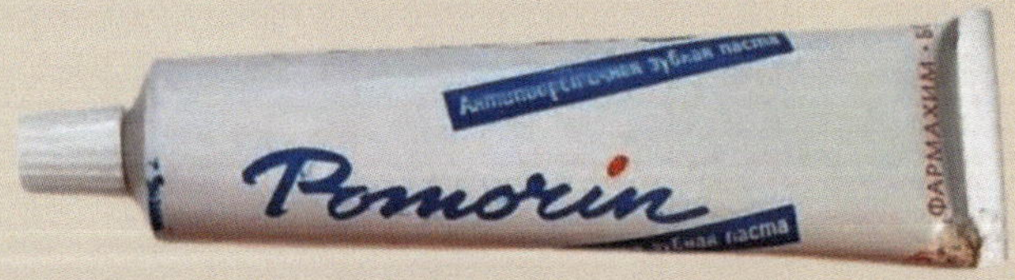

> 'The gunk contains ethanol, but eating it will make you vomit. Filter it through bread first - it absorbs the good stuff.' - Anonymous (Interview)

BF-6 Glue

Alcohol Content: ???%

A medical adhesive used to strengthen alcoholic beverages.

Fact: Nicknamed 'Boris Fedorovich', BF glue was used by conscripts and civilians alike.

Method

To separate the spirits from the adhesive one would insert a drill into a container of BF and stir slowly. The denser resin would remain on the stick, leaving the spirits in the can.

> 'Everyone became a chemistry master and they somehow managed to create spirits from car brake fluid, 'BF' glue, polish, tooth powder, and so on'.
> - Vladimir Bukovsky, *To Build a Castle*

Shoe Polish

Alcohol Content: ???%

Generally unsafe to consume, some shoe polishes are more hazardous than others.

Fact: Most contain ethylene glycol.

Method

- Spread a layer on bread. Put it onto a glass of water overnight and in the morning toss the bread and drink the water.

- Smear on bread and let it bake in the sun until the alcohol separates from the shoe polish. Then scrape the polish off and eat the bread. It would get you drunk.

“ ‘Smells like gas, tastes like gum’
- Anonymous ”

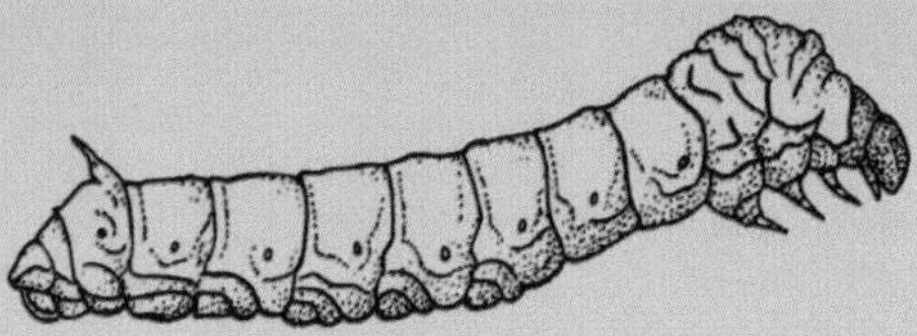

Insect Repellent

Alcohol Content: ???%

Alcohol mixed with toxins to repel bugs—insecticide was also consumed.

Fact: Diclofos, a household insecticide, was used recreationally. It changes the DNA of bacteria.

Method

Often sprayed from the can directly into a glass of beer in two or three shot bursts.

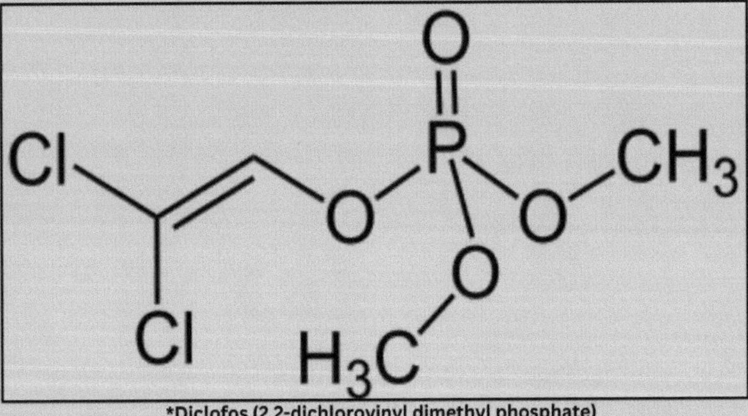

*Diclofos (2,2-dichlorovinyl dimethyl phosphate)

> ‘Out in the provinces, when there was beer, they couldn't resist strengthening it. For a few extra kopecks, three sprays of insect repellent were added to your mug.’
> - Daniel Genis, *Vice News*

T MEMT

Air Freshener

Alcohol Content: ???%

An aerosol can of isopropyl alcohol mixed with scented oils.

Fact: Unlike cologne, air freshener needed to be processed before heavy drinking.

Method

‘A small hole was punched in the can with a nail; 15 minutes later, all the pressurized gas would have escaped, allowing the can to be cut open. The contents would then be left to rest for an hour. After salt and water were added, and the sediment removed, the potion would be ready to drink.’

*Isopropyl Alcohol

“‘The smell often didn’t match the taste’
- Anonymous”

Pure Ethanol

Alcohol Content: 100%

A highly concentrated alcohol used primarily for cleaning.

Fact: Pure ethanol was high-quality stuff, often used by higher-ranking officers and medics.

Method

Watered down with flavored drinks like juice and kvass - a fermented cereal-based low-alcohol beverage.

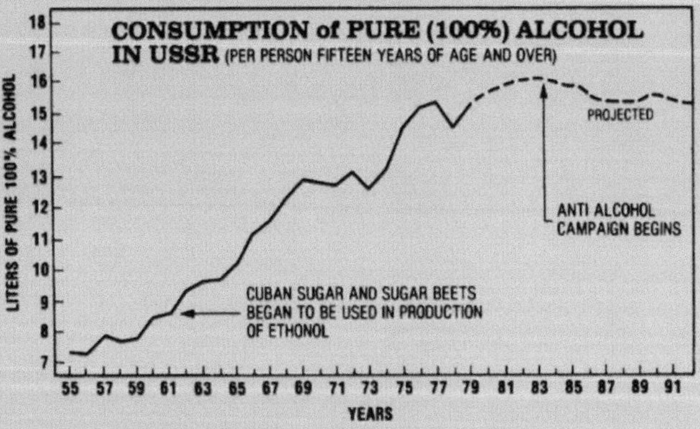

> 'The officers drank the surgical spirit, so we had to use petrol to clean the wounds' - Nurse, *Zinky Boys*

'Drinking people cause much trouble'
Yang, A. Chernomordik. 1929

‘Red-Head’

Alcohol Content: 40%+

The rust-infused dregs taken from the bottom of a supply tank carrying technical alcohol.

Fact: The last 200 liters of technical alcohol (used for cleaning or industrial work) would be disposed of by the manufacturer.

Method

Syphon the remaining alcohol out of a tanker transport container. At best, the liquid would be filtered through the rolled-up sleeves of an old quilted cotton jacket into which the rail car funnel would be inserted.

> ‘Queues of residents from nearby villages would form ready with buckets for this alcohol with a metallic taste’
> - Anonymous

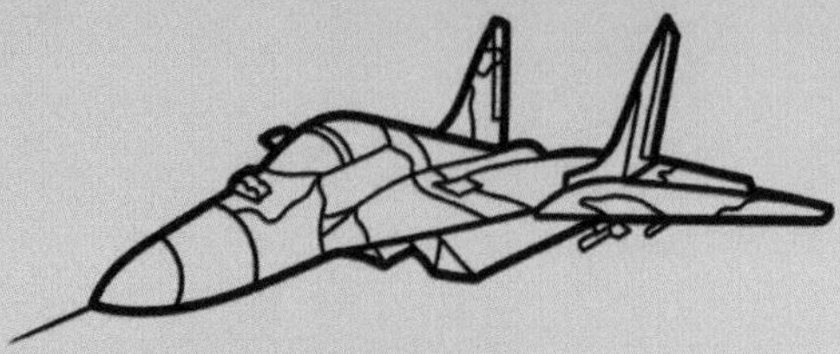

‘The Delicatessen’

Alcohol Content: 40%+

The MiG-25 contained a cooling system full of flight alcohol. Nicknamed the ‘gastronom’ (delicatessen).

Fact: The plane had the highest alcohol-to-pilot ratio of all Soviet aircraft. (300L/1 Pilot)

Method

During pre- and post-flight checks, the landing crew and pilots would have access to the coolant mix, which required frequent changing. It was better to take this pre-flight because after the liquid had traveled around the plane, it tasted of rubber and metal.

> ‘After swallowing down firewater, never breathe before chasing it with some water. The alcohol dries out the throat instantly, and breathing without re-moistening causes a brutal burning sensation' - Daniel Genis, *Vice News*

‘Supersonic Booze Cruze’

40% Ethyl Alcohol, 60% Distilled Water

The Tu-22 contained a massive amount of alcohol used as a refrigerant for the air conditioning system.

Fact: This bomber contained the highest alcohol content of all Soviet aircraft (400L).

Method

Take a hose and syphon alcohol from the coolant tank.

> ‘The mixture used for the Tu-22 was the same as that used in Soviet vodka’ - PaperSkiesAviation

295

ABSINTHE

‘Landing Gear Liqueur’

70% Glycerin, 20% Ethyl Alcohol, 10% Water

A thick, sweet fluid sipped by Soviet airmen which also functioned as a minor laxative.

Fact: The alcohol prevented the fluid from freezing and the addition of glycerin made the liquid thicker and more adhesive.

Method

Take the mixture and add it to a container. Mix it well to avoid laxative effects. Add flavoring—raspberry was a favorite. Enjoy straight at airfield temperature.

> ‘While liqueur was typically a women's drink, improper mixing of the liquid could cause a laxative effect. This element of risk and uncertainty made landing gear more of a drink for real men’ - PaperSkiesAviation

The Creation of 'Landing Gear Liqueur'

'Chronicle of a Dive Bomber, 1967'

'Sooltyga'

30% Ethyl Alcohol, 70% Water

A critical brake fluid in the Sukhoi SU-15 (1965).

Fact: The alcohol was developed to address the high breaking speed of the aircraft (350km/hour).

Method

Take a hose and syphon the brake fuel tank on the aircraft. Fill several flasks with the sooltyga to a maximum of 7.5 liters when changing fluid.

> 'The drink was typically enjoyed by younger flight personnel, while senior aviators enjoyed stronger stuff'
> - PaperSkiesAviation

'Shylo'

95.6% Ethyl Alcohol, 4.4% Water

A cooling mixture used for the Sukhoi SU-15's radar systems which frequently overheated.

Fact: In cooling systems, alcohol absorbs heat and evaporates—cooling things down—before being vented out via an exit point.

Method

Take a hose and syphon the 20-liter coolant tank. Pre-flight alcohol was considered to be of higher quality. There was more of it and it tasted better. The best time to get shylo was during pre-flight ground checks where—in a test of the systems—some liquid would drain onto the tarmac.

> 'Technicians usually poured used alcohol back into the container while keeping the new alcohol for themselves'
> - PaperSkiesAviation

'Shpaga'

40% Ethyl Alcohol, 60% Water

A cooling mixture used for Sukhoi SU-15s and various MiG radar systems.

Fact: Shpaga is the Russian word for Épée, a reference to the long metal ruler used to measure coolant levels.

Method

Take a hose and syphon the coolant tank.

Épée

"'In French, Épée means sword, while the Russian word for sword is сабля (sablya). While the former refers to a rapier, the latter describes a saber'.
- Joseph Ehrlich (Master Translator)"

‘Massandra’

50% Ethyl Alcohol, 50% Water

A drink produced by the MiG-25 fighter nicknamed the ‘Twin-Tail Restaurant’.

Fact: The name originates from a brand of popular Ukrainian wines from Crimea.

Method

Take a hose and siphon to the coolant tank. Take the alcohol home in containers.

> ‘Pilots stole so much alcohol that they ran out of bottles and containers. It was common to hear of bathtubs being used to store the stuff instead’. - PaperSkiesAviation

Posters

Anti-drinking propaganda

‘Socially Dangerous!’

All images courtesy of Radio Free Europe/Radio Liberty and The National Library of Scotland

'Got drunk, cursed, broke a little tree—it is shameful now to look people in the face.'

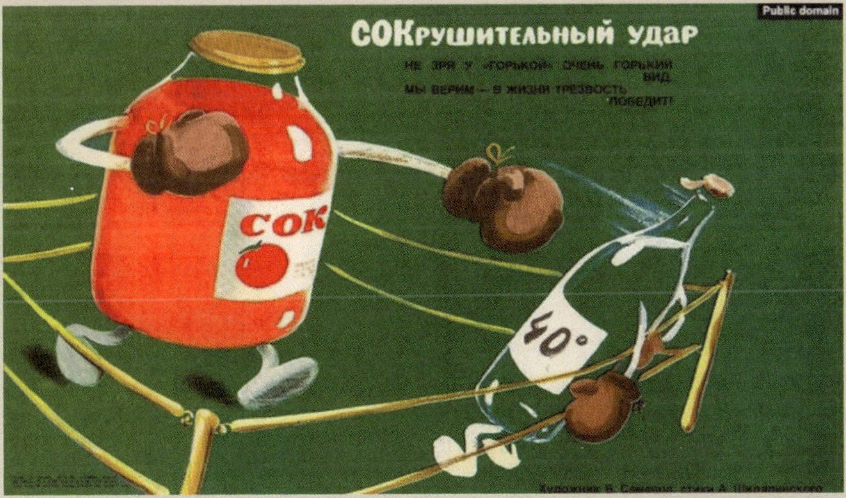

'Tomato juice delivers a knockout blow to a bottle of vodka.'

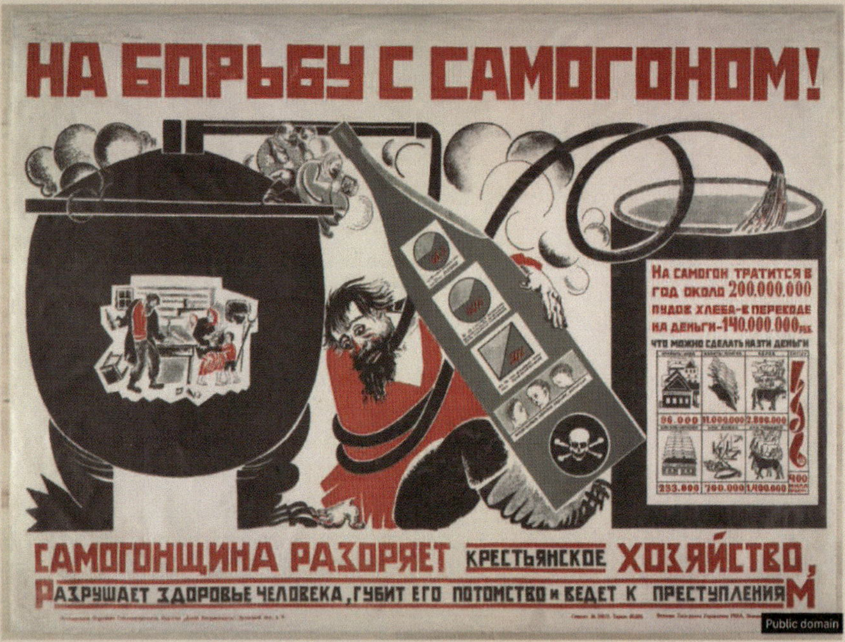

'To fight against moonshine!'

'Moonshining destroys peasant farming, undermines human health, ruins future generations, and leads to crime.'

'Either, Or.'

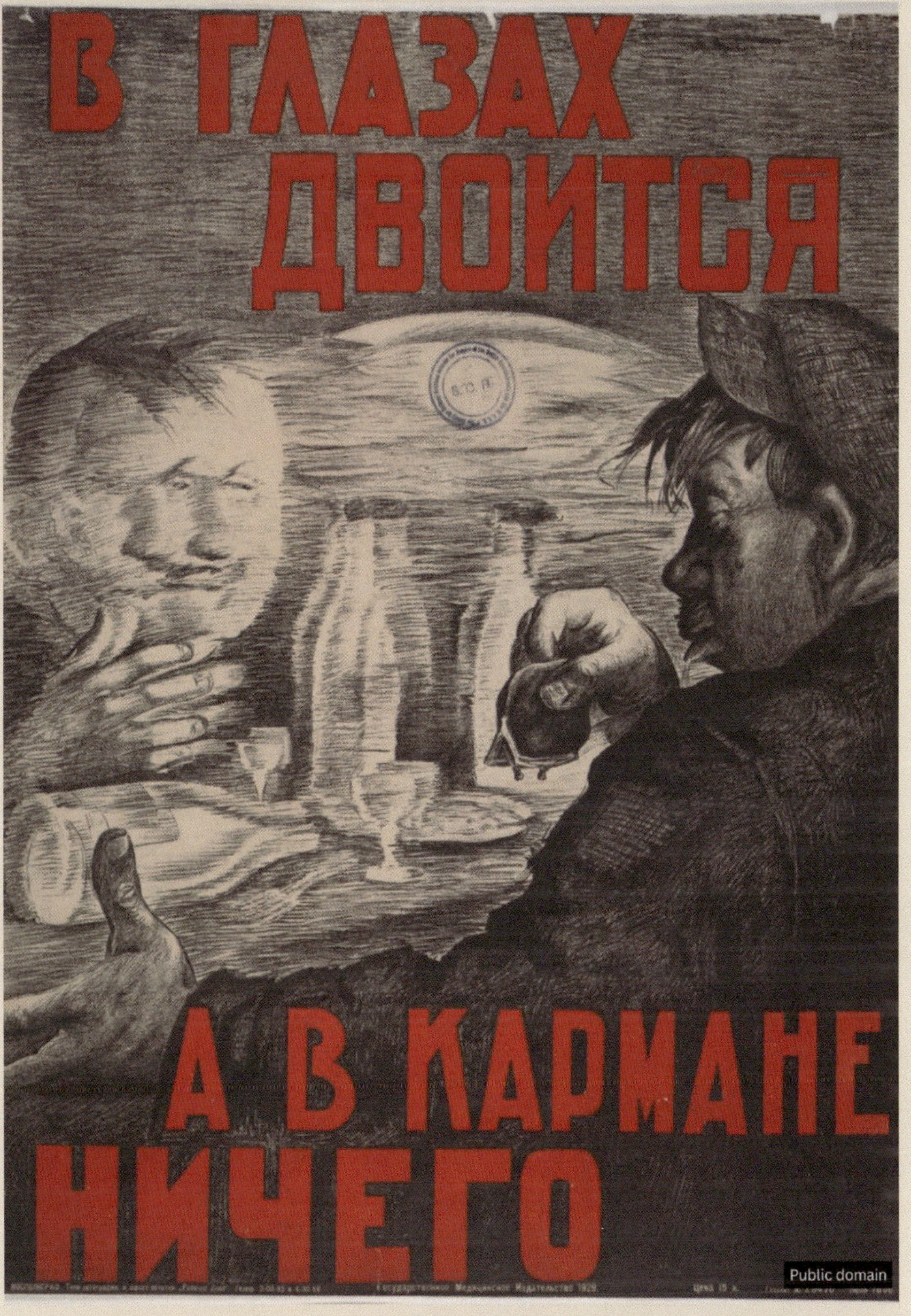

'You're seeing two of everything but in your pocket there's nothing' 1929.

'Sobriety is the norm of life'
Postage stamp, 1985.

‘A thimble, a shot, a glass, and a hooligan is created’

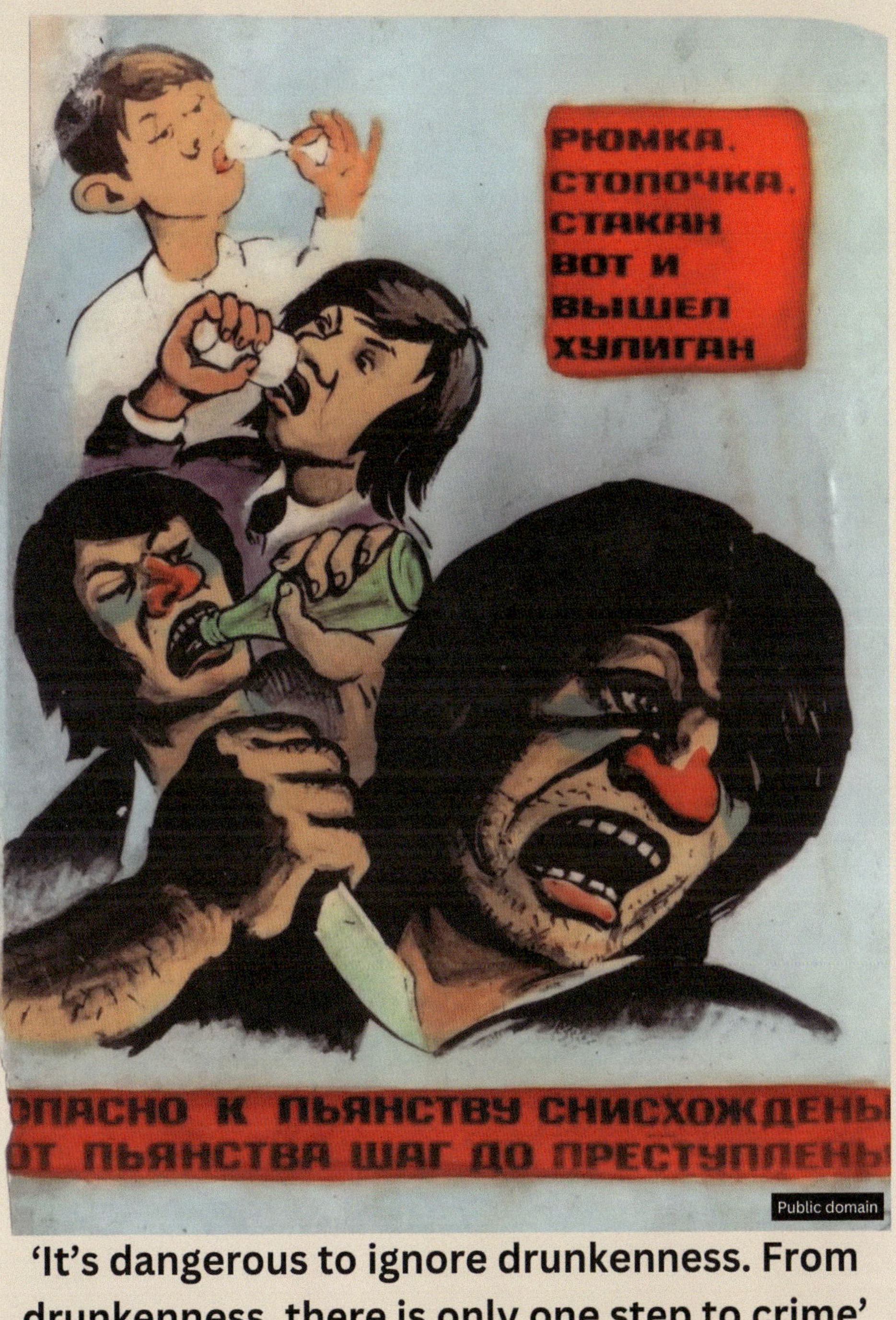

‘It’s dangerous to ignore drunkenness. From drunkenness, there is only one step to crime’

'And they say that we are pigs...' 1958.

Public domain

'This new look suits me.'

The poster shows a bottle tearing off a label for fortified white wine and replacing it with one for 'natural juice.'

‘We will expel the drinkers from the workplace!’

The bottle is labeled ‘Vodka’ and the pipe ‘Defect’, 1966.

'What miracles are done to my gate by my old friends: cigarette and vodka.'

COCKTAILS

simply undrinkable

UNHEALTHLY LIFESTYLE CHAPTER

Description

A boot beverage with a shiny twist. Introducing "Pavlov's Polish" – a Soviet-inspired blend of star anise and boot polish essence. Crafted for comrades, this flavorful potion salutes the discipline of parades with a surprising twist. Share laughter and solidarity with this whimsical sipper.

Get your shine on!

Pavlov's Polish

Ingredients

- 200 ml cognac (for resilience)
- 25 ml cointreau
- 25 ml lemon juice, plus a lemon wedge for the glass
- 4 cardamom pods, bruised
- 1 cinnamon stick
- 1 star anise
- Sliced ginger

Method

Take a sanitized boot receptacle and load it with dry ingredients. This will act as your mixer. Next, place a slice of rye bread on the shoe entrance and slowly pour the liquid through. Mix the cocktail in the toe of the boot. Glaze the entrance with sugar and add a lemon wedge, ginger, and a cinnamon stick for presentation.

Adorn with ice.

Description

A smooth blend of flight vodka and improvised bitters. Crafted for those who appreciate the finer altitudes of mixology, this high-flying concoction mirrors the precision of a well-executed flight. Elevate your spirits and take the war to the bugs with every sip.

Aviators Aftershave

Ingredients

- 50 ml shpaga (vodka)
- 2 tsp Cuban beet sugar
- Dash of hot water
- 2 sprays of insecticide (bitters)
- Orange zest
- 1 tsp honey
- 1/2 grapefruit
- Mint, blueberries, cucumber, and cherries

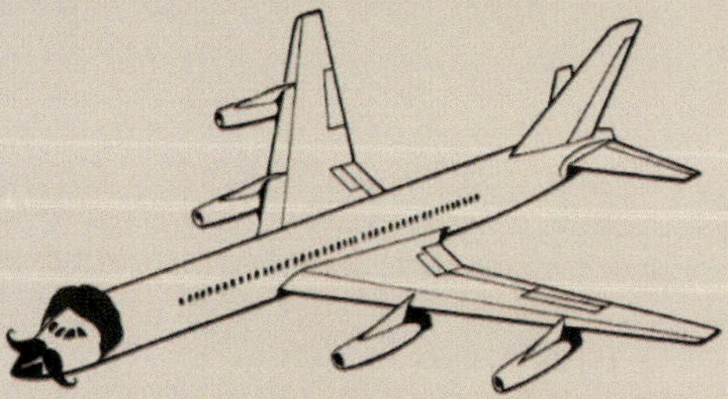

Method

Take two ladles of Shpaga from your bathtub home reserve. Add to a mason jar and let the sugar dissolve in. Next, give the mixture two bursts of insecticide (a dash of bitters). Mix with a dash of hot water and garnish with a runway of orange zest and grapefruit juice.

Decorate with mint, blueberries, sliced cumber, and whole cherries.

Description

A unique elixir designed to repel not just the summer heat but also unwanted insect invaders. Blending the robust flavors of kvass and beer with a burst of citrus and mint, this cocktail stands as a formidable bug deterrent. Say 'cheers' to a bug-free and delightfully cool experience!

Bolshevik Crawler

Ingredients

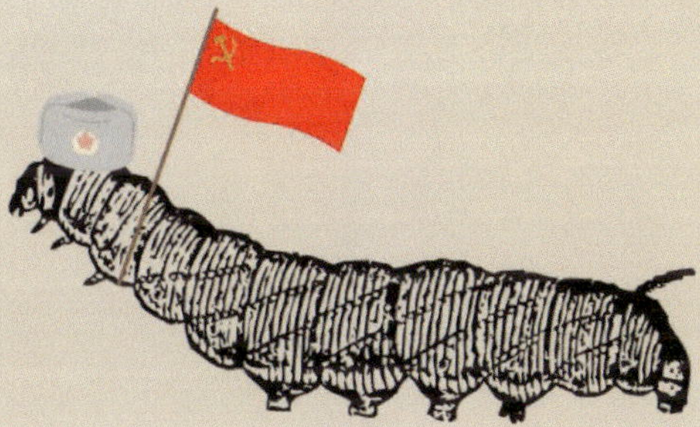

- 1 cup kvass
- 1 bottle of light beer
- 50 ml fresh lemon juice
- 2 sprays of insecticide (bitters)
- 25 ml simple syrup
- 1 tsp honey
- Fresh mint leaves
- Bay leaves, cherries, and sliced cucumber

Method

Take a cup of kvass (ideally from Poland), and mix it in a bucket with a bottle of cheap light beer. Add two shots of lemon juice, with two sprays of your favorite domestic insecticide (bitters). Add a shot of syrup and a bit of honey to improve the taste. Garnish with mint and bay leaves of the floral variety.

Toss in cherries and a cucumber for a post drink snack.

Description

Introducing 'Comrade Clean', a cocktail that channels the invigorating essence of your favorite toothpaste into a delightful adult beverage. Served over ice, this toothpaste-inspired elixir promises a cool, revitalizing experience, minus the dental work. Sip and savor the unique twist on freshness in this playful and palate-pleasing libation.

Comrade Clean

Ingredients

- 1 cup watermelon juice
- 25 ml mint grenadine syrup
- 25 ml fresh orange juice
- 50 ml citrus vodka
- 25 ml peppermint schnapps
- 1 tsp honey
- Fresh mint leaves
- Crushed ice

Method

Take an old mason jar and fill it with a cup of squeezed watermelon juice. Add mint grenadine and orange juice concoction to the container. Now embalm the mixture with citrus vodka and peppermint schnapps. Add a helping of honey and stir before tossing the brew with ice.

Enjoy cold, before bed.

Description

Introducing 'Comrade Cohesion', a glue themed cocktail that binds flavors in solidarity. This adhesive elixir boasts a smooth and potent profile. Served over ice and garnished with a subtle nod to the iconic hammer and sickle, "Comrade Cohesion" is a toast to shared resilience and enduring connections.

Comrade Cohesion

Ingredients

- 25 ml gin
- 25 ml sweet vermouth
- 25 ml campari
- Orange slice
- Ice

Method

Take an old samovar and add your gin, vermouth, and campari. Mix with a spoon and add an orange slice and ice for visual appreciation. Use the spigot to extract your beverage and enjoy it at room temperature.

Description

A cocktail that blends the cold austere environment of the Soviet penal system with a warm empowering sipper embodying the much-loved Chifir tea. Kick back in your cell, heat up the hotplate, and fend off starvation with this classic punitive drink.

Gulag Grip Libation

Ingredients

- 60 ml black tea
- 60 ml dark rum
- 300 ml orange juice
- 150 ml lemon juice
- Orange garnish

Method

Take a pot and add black tea leaves. With 60 ml of water, boil the tea three times over two hours. Then add dark rum, followed by orange and lemon juice. Rewarm the liquid before drinking, and add cinnamon, chocolate, and star anise for decoration.

Description

A chilling concoction that takes inspiration from the cool efficiency of antifreeze. As smooth as a well-maintained engine, this frigid potation is served over ice with a twist of lemon, it's a refreshing tribute to cool efficiency

Fyodor Freezer

Ingredients

- 50 ml bourbon whiskey
- 25 ml lemon juice
- 25 ml simple syrup
- Orange or lemon peel
- Cocktail Cherry

Method

Take a shallow metal cup and mix the liquids. Place the container in the freezer or in outside freezing conditions for twenty minutes before consumption. Add an orange or lemon peel and a cocktail cherry for decoration.

Note: You can adjust the sweetness levels to fit your taste.

'WILL YOU BE THE THIRD?'

WARNING

THIS WORK INCORPORATED ELEMENTS OF HISTORICAL FICTION. ACCOUNTS OF SUBSTANCE ABUSE ARE ACCURATE, WHILE RECENT DRINK ADAPTATIONS ARE FICTION. IT IS UNSAFE TO CONSUME ANY UNREGULATED SUBSTANCE.

DO NOT DRINK GLUE

KE&RA, Georgian Restaurant - Gori, Georgia

In addition to his appreciation of DIY alcohol, the author (above) holds an MA and MLitt from the University of St Andrews with a focus on the Soviet-Afghan War and Russian military culture.

He is the director of Blue Sky Career Aid, an NGO that helps refugees find employment in the United Kingdom. All funds raised through book sales are used for charitable purposes.

Printed in Great Britain
by Amazon

38729956R00037